Maiolica, Delft and Faïence

Maiolica, Delft and Faïence

Giuseppe Scavizzi

HAMLYN

Translated by Peter Locke from the Italian original

Maioliche dal Rinascimento ad aggi

©*1966 Fratelli Fabbri Editori, Milan*

This edition © *1970*
THE HAMLYN PUBLISHING GROUP LIMITED
LONDON · NEW YORK · SYDNEY · TORONTO
Hamlyn House, Feltham, Middlesex, England

SBN 600359190

Text filmset by Filmtype Services, Scarborough, England.

Printed in Italy by Fratelli Fabbri Editori, Milan

Bound in Scotland by Hunter and Foulis Ltd., Edinburgh

Contents

INTRODUCTION

The arts for the most part evolve continuously, without serious breaks in their history. There is, however, one important and well-marked break in the history of ceramics. On one side are ceramics which, however luxurious, were evidently intended for some particular use, either domestic or decorative; on the other are pieces which manifest a search for an independent form dictated only by the work itself. The latter development took place during the Renaissance, and as a result ceramic art acquired the importance and dignity that it had previously possessed in the Middle East, and particularly in the Islamic World.

This occurred in the important type of pottery known as tin-glazed earthenware. Tin-glaze, sometimes known as tin-enamel is so called because the addition of tin oxide to the lead-glaze produces an opaque, white, enamel-like surface which can be effectively decorated by painting with oxides or enamel colours. Originally the same high temperature firing was used to fuse the white background glaze and to reveal the designs painted on in a limited number of colours based on copper, metallic oxides, cobalt, manganese, antimony and iron – which were able to withstand the great heat. Later, as techniques became

European Centres for the
manufacture of Maiolica,
Delft and Faience

Eckernförde

Mors

MARK

Copenhagen

Kastrup

Kiel

Kellinghusen

Stockelsdorff

Hamburg

GERMANY

Warsaw

Brunswick · Berlin

POLAND

Potsdam

Magedeburg

Kassel · Dresden

Frankfurt

BOHEMIA

Bayreuth · Prague

Höchst

Moravia

Nuremberg

Ludwigsburg

Holitsch Slovakia

Augsburg

AUSTRIA

Zurich · Innsbruck

Beromünster

HUNGARY

ZERLAND

RUMANIA

Bassano · Venezia

Milan

Padua

Bucharest ·

Ferrara

Lodi

Ravenna

guria

Romagna

Faenza

Genoa

Florence

Forlí

bisola · Pisa

Urbino

Pesaro

Tuscany

The Marches

Perugia

afaggiolo

Deruta

Montelupo

Umbria

Castelli

Siena

Abruzzi Lucera

Rome

Latium

Apulia

Gubbio

Orvieto

ITALY

Naples

Taranto

Palermo

Trapani

Sicily

Caltagirone

1   Luca della Robbia. Coat of arms of the Bartolini-Salimbeni in a garland of leaves and fruit. Museo Nazionale del Bargello, Florence.

1   Luca della Robbia. Coat of arms of the Bartolini-Salimbeni in a garland of leaves and fruit. Museo Nazionale del Bargello, Florence. Nothing heraldic and conventionalised in this coat of arms which, with its delicate rendering of fruit — fleshy and radiant with colour — appears to be one of the oldest examples of still-life in Italian art. These works of Luca were destined to revolutionise the whole scope of maiolica.

2   Florence. Plate with a woman's head. Mid 15th century. Victoria and Albert Museum, London. This is one of the oldest examples of Italian maiolica in which the ornamentation, which is still stylised, leaves room for a human head on the centrepiece. This portrait is drawn in fine, delicate lines in the manner of Verrocchio.

3   Faenza. Pharmaceutical jar with a young man's head, *c*. 1470–80. Victoria and Albert Museum, London. This too is a transitional work in that the figured area tends to dominate the ornamentation. In works of this kind figures are usually displayed on a white background reserved for them in the middle of the decoration. A balance between ornament and figure has not yet been achieved.

4   Faenza. Cup with 'Julia bela', *c*. 1500. Museo Internazionale delle Ceramiche, Faenza. A fine example of a very popular 16th-century piece, the 'loving cup'. These articles were presented on the occasion of engagements or simply as gifts to the beloved. The free strokes of the brush create a fresh female likeness; the style of this piece is more mature than that of the two preceding works.

2 Florence. Plate with a woman's head. Mid 15th century.
Victoria and Albert Museum, London.

3   Faenza. Pharmaceutical jar with a young man's head,
c. 1470-80. Victoria and Albert Museum, London.

IVLIA

BELA

4   Faenza. Cup with 'Julia bela', *c.*1500. Museo
Internazionale delle Ceramiche, Faenza.

more sophisticated a second firing was often used to add a decorative lustre, and in the 18th century, a second firing at a much lower temperature allowed the use of a greatly increased colour range. Tin-glazed ware is classified according to its place of manufacture: in Italy it is called 'maiolica', in Holland and England 'delftware', and in France and other European countries 'faïence'. The development described in the previous paragraph took place in the production of maiolica in Renaissance Italy.

ITALY
The Renaissance
Several factors contributed. First, pottery was more closely connected with everyday domestic life than any other kind of art. For this reason it was beneficially affected by the new value attributed by Renaissance man to private life – to both comfort and display.

Second, appreciation of the individual piece led to a sharper differentiation of styles. While Hispano-Moresque workshops, the most productive and highly esteemed of the late Middle Ages, were bringing out magnificent and valuable pieces that were nonetheless largely alike in their decorative motifs and in the colours employed, Italian craftsmen were producing new pieces that differed from one another very considerably. The individualism of the Renaissance was apparent here, in the taste of purchasers as well as makers.

Throughout the Middle Ages, even in the Arab world, the most splendid ceramic object was in the last resort no more than a decorative piece whose function was already determined. Exactly similar pieces might appear among household furnishings or in civil or religious buildings, their only purpose being to relieve the bareness of a wall with a splash of colour. In the Middle Ages there was a hierarchy in the arts as in all other areas of life. By contrast, Renaissance pottery displays a constant vitality and found increasing inspiration in other arts. Contacts with painting, sculpture and metalwork became closer as the years passed, and each form of art was deeply influenced by the others. The freedom with which pottery could develop changed it from a craft consisting of types and genres to an art produced by defined personalities.

All this of course happened gradually. It was only in the course of the Renaissance that the change became at all clear; and it was largely due to 15th-century Florentine craftsmen that the barriers which had hitherto separated the arts disappeared. The architect Brunelleschi, the sculptors Ghiberti, Donatello and Verrocchio, and the painter Pollaiuolo were all omnicompetent; and the many-sided genius of Alberti, Leonardo and Michelangelo is too well-known to require further comment. In the same way, the work of the great sculptor Luca della Robbia did much to bring about a revival of pottery. He accomplished this by the introduction of naturalistic motifs and, more important, by his superior understanding of the means to be employed. It was as a result of the increased possibilities in painting terracotta that craftsmen in maiolica working in Florence, Emilia and the Romagna introduced the human figure into their works. As a result of the new stimulus, by 1475 potters in Faenza were experimenting with round terracotta tablets, and creating Nativities and Depositions that combined a popular character with an intense devotional appeal.

Della Robbia first employed maiolica in order to introduce colour into his work as a sculptor, applying it in a way that gives his creations a detached, transcendent beauty. In time he applied it to the figures as well as the backgrounds, with a sparing use of colour, especially white and blue, that suggests a search for a highly spiritual type of beauty. For this reason della Robbia's art is outside the main line of development traced in this book.

5   Faenza. Plate with David. Early 16th century. Museo
Nazionale del Bargello, Florence.

5   Faenza. Plate with David. Early 16th century. Museo Nazionale del Bargello, Florence. A piece in a very refined style. The main figuration is matched with a border. The piece is imaginatively ornamented with the most fashionable motifs of contemporary painting: twists of acanthus, masks and armour. However, the decoration around the edge tends to predominate over the main figuration.

6   Faenza, the Pirota workshop. Plate with a figure of a woman. Museo Nazionale del Bargello, Florence. The fineness of detail is remarkable, as are the proportions of the various decorated areas, which have exact and fundamental relationships to each other. The decoration, a very personal elaboration of a grotesque theme, retains a trace of the Moorish linear style.

7   Faenza. Large plate with the figures of a woman and child. 16th century. Museo Internazionale delle Ceramiche, Faenza. The form of the bean-motif ornamentation and the new, more free style of painting foreshadow what were to become the typical patterns of 17th-century pottery.

8   Jacopo Fattorini. Plate with Judith. Victoria and Albert Museum, London. A fine example of the work produced at Cafaggiolo in about 1510. The slender, elegant figures and the almost heraldic pattern of the drapery blown by the wind reveal a stylistic connection with the youthful work of Raphael.

9   Cafaggiolo. Plate with fight scenes. 1515–20. By kind permission of the Fitzwilliam Museum, Cambridge. Plate in honour of a noble Florentine family. The borders include medallions; the scenes of heroes and centaurs fighting from a pattern symbolising the triumphs of the house.

6   Faenza, the Pirota workshop. Plate with a figure of a
woman. Museo Nazionale del Bargello, Florence.

7 Faenza. Large plate with the figures of a woman and child. 16th century. Museo Internazionale delle Ceramiche, Faenza.

8　Jacapo Fattorini. Plate with Judith. Victoria and Albert Museum, London.

9   Cafaggiolo. Plate with fight scenes. 1515-1520. By kind
permission of the Fitzwilliam Museum, Cambridge.

Della Robbia had broken the barrier that had previously separated ceramics from other arts. Luca's successors, his nephew Andrea and Andrea's son Giovanni, took up the art and used it for every kind of decoration, for instance in monumental figures such as Andrea's *Annunciation* of 1479 in the Chiesa della Verna and Giovanni's altar screen of 1521 in the Museo Nazionale, Florence, and in work that was purely ornamental such as coats of arms or garlands (often treated as a pretext for naturalistic depiction of still-life subjects).

Other Italian potters did not immediately follow the new paths opened up by della Robbia. For some time their efforts were primarily directed towards shaking off the old ornamental styles, and even in the last two decades of the 15th century both old and new styles co-existed in advanced artistic centres. Even now it is in many cases difficult to decide whether similarly decorated groups of pottery properly belong to the late Medieval tradition or are early products of the new ideas.

Some schools continued to model their decorative patterns on Eastern, Spanish or Gothic styles. Italo-Moresque ware, for example, was widely used in Tuscany throughout the second half of the 15th century. This and other groups belonged to the *stile severo* (severe style) which included the 'green family', the 'relief blue' and the 'diluted blue'. Even so, their design developed a much greater spatial feeling, to the point of including figures in high relief.

It was the workshops of Florence and Faenza that made the decisive move towards more modern styles. Their craftsmen created new themes in both design and decoration and freed themselves from preoccupation with traditional styles. After the middle of the 15th century, examples of the 'floral Gothic' style were painted in a new manner, and with colours of much greater intensity. Leaves, for instance, were still stylised but took on a new fleshiness and richness. Plates and *albarelli* (drugpots) often included portraits of women and children in contemporary clothing.

The potters of Faenza made complex, perfectly round pieces which attained the level of good popular craftsmanship. They brought new life to Italian pottery, and dated groups in the new manner appear regularly from 1477. Two Madonnas of 1477 are in London collections, and a Deposition of 1487 is in the Metropolitan Museum, New York. The intense religious feeling of these pieces suggests the influence of Niccolò dell'Arca, a sculptor from Apulia who created some moving Depositions on a grand scale in terracotta; the devotional intensity of his work – of a kind more common in northern European art – made followers throughout Emilia. It was from Faenza also that the first products (jugs, plates, etc.) came which had figuration, not necessarily religious, covering the entire surface, thereby eliminating the decorative motif around the edges. This is the origin of the *istoriate* piece with narrative subjects mainly taken from Classical mythology or the Bible; as we shall see, it was subsequently developed, particularly in Urbino, and became one of the glories of Italian pottery.

The lively taste for line and figure drawing displayed by Faenza craftsmen is explained, according to Ballardini's theory, by the appearance of painters in the workshops. This undoubtedly made for a constant and stimulating contact between the two arts. Similar examples of such contact may be seen in Tuscany, Umbria and elsewhere. As early as the mid 15th century, Florentine potters had begun to incorporate figures derived from works by the greatest contemporary artists into their products, and as time went on they intelligently followed the new forms in Botticellian style. Similarly, in Deruta and Urbino the potters responded to the forms of Perugino and Raphael, while the earliest pottery in Bologna and Ferrara reflects the twisting linear style of the masters of the latter city. The workshops of Faenza and Pesaro

10   Siena. Plate with St. Sebastian. 16th century Victoria
and Albert Museum, London.

10 Siena. Plate with St Sebastian. 16th century. Victoria and Albert Museum, London. This plate (*c*. 1510) comes from the workshop of Maestro Benedetto, and adheres to the manner of the school of Faenza. The delicately modelled picture of St. Sebastian recalls the works of Perugino.

11 Deruta. Plate with grotesques. 1525. Victoria and Albert Museum, London. At Deruta, as elsewhere, the variations were almost infinite. This plate, decorated with candelabras, sphinxes and dragons, affords a typical example of a fantastic play of forms, releasing at times a latent taste for surrealism. The grotesque can probably be said to have found wider expression in Renaissance maiolica than in painting itself.

12 Casteldurante. Plate with coat of arms. 16th century. Museo Civico, Bologna. Here are found in rich combination many of the themes beloved of the Renaissance: the candelabra, medallions with portraits busts, and armour. The craftsmen of Casteldurante, like those of Deruta, had a taste for rich, almost overabundant decoration – a taste that was to be developed even further at Urbino.

13 Casteldurante. Cup with Marfisa. 16th century. Museo Internazionale delle Ceramiche, Faenza. This type of 'loving cup' derives from Faenza. The woman's martial dress indicates her argumentative character, and the letters composing her name are set out in such a way as to suggest an allusion to Mars. Not infrequently these cups did in fact allude, seriously or jokingly, to the character of the person portrayed.

11   Deruta. Plate with grotesques. 1525 Victoria and Albert
Museum, London.

12   Casteldurante. Plate with coat of arms. 16th century.
Museo Civico, Bologna.

·MAR·FI   SA^A

13 Casteldurante. Cup with Marfisa. 16th century. Museo
Internazionale delle Ceramiche, Faenza.

also adopted the miniaturistic forms and intense colours of the Bianchi of Ferrara.

In the first twenty years of the 16th century the motifs and style of the Raphaelite school, which had become familiar through the prints of Marcantonio, spread remarkably rapidly, and were incorporated wholesale into the most splendid dishes, and the grotesque – the principal kind of decoration in the 16th century – made a triumphant entry into every kind of work. Other equally familiar motifs (such as trophies of arms, dolphins playing, and musical instruments) came from the painted façades of Venice and Rome. In addition, motifs of cherubs by Donatello were exploited, as were the prints of Mantegna and Dürer. An art which presumed to take over masterpieces of other mediums – to reduce the works of Raphael to a size no larger than the palm of a hand – ran the risk of betraying its own functions, despite the skill of its executants, and indeed the limit beyond which an art loses its individual quality was sometimes passed.

The masters of maiolica in effect became distributors of culture through their *istoriate* style. At first their work fell into two distinct categories, 'popular' and 'cultured'; but soon it was directed indiscriminately at every class: the rich, the poor, the bourgeois, and the great and lesser nobility. Maiolica works pleased high and low alike, without becoming mere ancillaries of the 'major' arts because craftsmen created new decorative ideas (new colours, lustre) and developed characteristic forms. A convincing indication of the role of maiolica is the fact that the shops that supplied ceramic hospital equipment also supplied pieces to popes and princes.

Faenza and its rivals

From the middle of the 15th century, and particularly between 1470 and 1500, the artists of Florence and Faenza left large white spaces, 'reserves', in the middle of their plates in which they drew elegant portraits of young men, scenes of daily life, proverbial situations, coats of arms and heraldic devices. Literary themes of triumphs and allegories of life also appeared. This great variety of themes, which also included religious subjects, was largely due to the destination of the articles – plates, cups and jugs – which were presented as gifts at births, marriages and other festive occasions.

This style, in which the delineation is somewhat crude and the figures are juxtaposed but not joined, was succeeded about 1500 by that of the 'Individual Masters' of Faenza. By means of richer, warmer colouring and a new, more unified idea of decoration, they achieved results which were for the first time quite distinct from the Medieval style. The artist's descriptive vein could find freer expression with this richer painting and, as the name of the style implies, he could fashion an individuality which made him distinct from every other artist. This makes for easier classification, and works by various groups or individual artists can be distinguished, for example 'The Master of St John', 'The Master of the Resurrection' (some of whose works are in the Victora and Albert Museum), 'The Master of Selene', 'The Painter of the Assunta' and the monogrammist 'B. T.' Some of these earliest masters were distinguished by their spontaneity, and were often amazingly successful in capturing intimate scenes of everyday life which painting achieved only later.

One of the most important Faenzan workshops was that of Casa Pirota. From the first decade of the 16th century it issued plates splendidly decorated with *istoriate* scenes, grotesques on an azure enamel ground, and abstract geometrical motifs somewhat reminiscent of Chinese porcelain and foreshadowing the styles of Rouen and Moustiers. Other important workshops were those of the brothers Piero and Paolo Bergantini and of Giuliano and Sebastiano Manara, while that of Virgilio Calamelli specialised in the production of fluted dishes decorated by quarters with stylised leaves in ochre and blue. Faenza was clearly the most

14 Urbino. Trencher. 16th century. Museo Internazionale delle Ceramiche, Faenza.

15 Francesco Xanto Avelli. Plate with Joseph and Potiphar's wife. Museo Nazionale del Bargello, Florence.

16 Urbino. Plate with Leda. 16th century. Museo Nazionale del Bargello, Florence.

14 Urbino. Trencher. 16th century. Museo Internazionale delle Ceramiche, Faenza. This trencher was originally part of a service made for the wedding of a member of the Gonzaga family; hence the subject, which combines allusions to the triumph of Mars and the power of love. It displays all the distinctive Classical grace of the *istoriate* style of Urbino.

15 Francesco Xanto Avelli. Plate with Joseph and Potiphar's wife. Museo Nazionale del Bargello, Florence. A superb example of the work of a master from Urbino; its inspiration is the work of Raphael, particularly the Vatican Loggias. The school of Urbino greatly extended the possibilities of colouring pottery: research into ranges of colour most closely similar to those of painting led to the discovery of new colours of a more splendid richness and intensity.

16 Urbino. Plate with Leda. 16th century. Museo Nazionale del Bargello, Florence. As the century advanced, the school of Urbino developed a richer style of decoration, extending the traditional repertory of the grotesque with figures taken from mythology and – as in this example – with the free juxtaposition of the most diverse subjects: cherubs, armed men, dogs and birds. The result is magnificent and bears comparison with the best works by silversmiths and goldsmiths.

17 Urbino. Plate with the Manna falling from Heaven. 16th century. Museo Nazionale del Bargello, Florence. Here too is an example of the *istoriate* style in which the Classicism of the figures reverts to the manner of Raphael. The most frequently repeated subjects were the myths and history of antiquity.

17 Urbino. Plate with the Manna falling from Heaven. 16th century. Museo Nazionale del Bargello, Florence.

influential school in the Italian Renaissance. From it came Maestro Benedetto, the principal exponent of the Sienese School, and Zoan Maria, founder of the school of Casteldurante, as well as the makers of the famous pavements of S. Petronio in Bologna (Capella Vaselli, 1487) and S. Sebastiano in Venice (Capella Lando, 1570).

Cafaggiolo developed the *istoriate* style slightly later. It was the ancient centre of Tuscan maiolica and again became famous in the early part of the 16th century, through the distinguished work of Pietro and Stefano Fattorini, who had been called there from the earliest workshop of all (Montelupo) by Pierfrancesco de Medici. In 1507 Pietro died, and it was one of his sons, Jacopo, who helped Stefano in the work of reviving maiolica production. Cafaggiolo also produced work decorated with grotesques, allegories of love and subjects of a general religious nature. Its craftsmen also used an intense range of colour in a style (characteristic of the first phase of the Renaissance) which came to be known as the *stile bello* ('beautiful style'). The art of Cafaggiolo differs from that of Faenza in that its decoration is richer and its style slightly more elevated. Only occasionally does it lean towards as stylised, as spontaneous, and as impressionistic a manner as that of the school of Faenza. A fine example is the superlative dish of about 1510 (Victoria and Albert Museum), on which the artist himself is portrayed in the act of painting an engaged couple. Incidentally, it should be remembered that articles from the same workshop do not always show the same stylistic traits. Workshops in fact, employed potters and painters of different schools who sometimes came from great distances and, if their skill was exceptional, moved from one workshop to another.

Cafaggiolo ware did not evolve with time, and the only new decorative types produced in the middle of the 16th century were imitations of Chinese porcelain similar to those being produced in other parts of Italy (notably in the Marches and the Veneto). In Florence these efforts acquired a special value thanks to the great interest shown by the Medici in research into the making of porcelain. This culminated in the 1570s with the discovery of what is known today as 'Medici porcelain'.

Many other workshops were extremely active in this period and were achieving notable results by the use of different technical procedures, colours and lustres, as well as by different artistic concepts. The most noteworthy were the workshops of Montelupo and Siena in Tuscany, Deruta and Gubbio in Umbria, Pesaro in the Marches, Forli and Ferrara in Emilia,

Padua and Venice in the Veneto, and Rome, Naples and Trapani further south.

The Sienese school was not highly original, but it is remembered for a few outstanding works – such as the floor of the Cappella Bichi in S. Agostino (1488) and the floor of the Libreria Piccolomini (1507) – and for the work of certain masters like Benedetto di Giorgio, who came from Faenza. A plate of his of 1541 is now in the Victoria and Albert Museum.

The schools of Deruta and Gubbio were more original, particularly in developing lustres (colours made from finely ground particles of metal), which had until that time been a Hispano-Moresque speciality. Giorgio Andreoli, known as Maestro Giorgio, worked at Gubbio during the first half of the century. In addition to making pieces in his own workshops, he used his lustres (varying from red to golden yellow and turquoise) to put the finishing touches to pieces sent to him by the best artists of the time. Some new forms, such as the wide vase in the shape of a pine cone and the cup with straight sides, were invented at Deruta. At both Deruta and Gubbio some kind of decoration in light relief was frequently superimposed on a piece. This not only heightened the effect of the glaze but also produced a subtle interplay of reflections of light from the surface.

18 Urbino. Vase. 16th century. Galleria Estense, Modena.

18   Urbino. Vase. ¹ ₋ın century. Galleria Estense, Modena. Made like other no less monumental pieces for Alfonso II d'Este. The richness of the modelling and the courtly ornamentation show that it was intended to match the magnificent furnishing of a noble, late Renaissance palace. At this time maiolica performed the function that porcelain was to have in the 18th century.

19   Venice. Tray. 16th century. Museo Internazionale Ceramiche, Faenza. In the 16th century Venetian workshops generally showed a freer attitude towards Classical themes, combining motifs of various origins in a fanciful ensemble. Even pictorially they attempted a closer blend and a warmer tone, as in the works of Maestro Ludovico and Giovan Domenico.

20   Montelupo. Plate with the figure of a soldier, *c.* 1630. Victoria and Albert Museum, London. A typical product of the Tuscan factory, the range of which in the 17th century was limited to a few genre themes depicted with a strong feeling for burlesque. Much of its ware is commonplace.

21   Albisola. Plate with the figures of armed men. 17th century. Museo del Castello Sforzesco, Milan. The oldest maiolica of Liguria is distinctive because of its swift, flowing style of painting, which owes a good deal to the *compendiario* style of the 16th-century masters of Faenza. The subjects are often inspired (though only vaguely) by Classical antiquity, with figures of divinities or armed cavaliers, but explicit references to history or mythology are avoided.

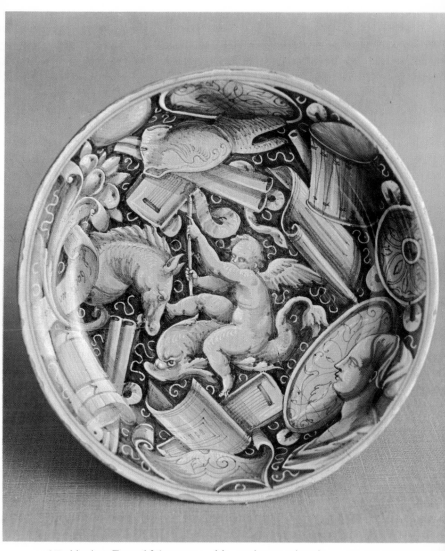

19 Venice. Tray. 16th century. Museo Internazionale Ceramiche, Faenza.

20 Montelupo. Plate with the figure of a soldier, *c.*1630.
Victoria and Albert Museum, London.

21 Albisola. Plate with the figures of armed men. 17th
century. Museo del Castello Sforzesco, Milan.

The 16th-century Italian centre in which the *istoriate* style reached its zenith was Urbino, whose products exerted great influence throughout Europe well into the following century. Urbino was the logical successor to Casteldurante, since it was founded by the family of Nicolò Pellipario, who moved there in 1528. Pellipario, who some consider the greatest maiolica painter of the Renaissance, had been taught at Casteldurante by Zoan Maria, who came from Faenza. Pellipario created plates the whole surface of which was decorated with subjects drawn from chivalry, Classical antiquity and grotesques. He had evidently studied the prints of his time carefully, especially those of the school of Raphael. Some of his renowned services are among the greatest Renaissance representations of mythical and fabulous scenes, achieved by means of an amazing interpretative ability and a delicate palette. Outstanding examples are the services in the Museo Correr in Venice, made for the Ridolfi-Medici in 1515, and that of 1528 made for Isabella d'Este Gonzaga. Pellipario's Classical sense of proportion was a great influence on his pupils, and is characteristic of Urbino ware. Francesco Xanto Avelli brought the *istoriate* style to Classical dimensions and devoted himself to a 'Roman' kind of decoration, often reproducing the scenes and compositions of Raphael and his school. Pellipario's family (who took the name Fontana) and Antonio Patanazzi worked in this style with a dignity which at times verges on the pompous; the best of their services was made for Guidobaldo della Rovere.

The originality of the craftsmen of Urbino lay not only in the painters' use of the *istoriate* style, but also in the creativity of the potters. The way in which the painters of Renaissance maiolica assimilated contemporary painting shows their participation in the art of the time; and it is evident from the shapes of the wares that the potters paid equally close attention to the art of the silversmith. At the end of the 15th century plates and mugs were still being made in shapes that had been used for decades; but during the 16th century the potters of Faenza brought greater variety to their creations by means of the continuous moulded treatment of every detail. Fluted plates, for example, were inspired by a particular type of metal dish, German in origin, which was widely found in Italy. Cups, bowls and medicinal jars and jugs similarly displayed the influence of works in silver or beaten copper, in which the Venetians in particular were highly skilled. Many plates were fashioned with fine layers of clay raised along the edge in obvious imitation of silverware. Sometimes the work was *a barbottina* (with parts stuck on in relief) reminiscent of similar work in metal. The superb showpieces which come from the workshops of Pellipario and the Fontanas demonstrate their desire to bring maiolica into competition with metalwork. Artists of the time, especially painters, were familiar with antique works, and this knowledge encouraged the creation of vases with smooth, elegant lines on high bases with twisted handles. Information about Classical pottery came either directly from archaeological discoveries or through representations of pieces in newly-discovered Classical pictures, for instance wide three-cornered fruit bowls standing upon modelled lions' paws. Urbino maiolica attained a sublime richness of colour in the *istoriate* pieces, and a formal splendour typical of mature Renaissance art. If the plates of Cafaggiolo and Faenza bring to mind the paintings of Raphael, the tall vases of Urbino may justly be compared with the works of Perin del Vaga and Salviati.

With the school of Urbino maiolica reached its highest peak of grandeur and it made a great impact on the schools of the following century by virtue of the inventive inspiration of its modelled and decorative elements.

Towards the end of the 16th century Faenza again became the leading centre, its craftsmen developing a new decorative style which returned to simpler and more immediate forms of expression. The two outstanding masters of this art, both active in the latter part of the 16th century, were Vergiliotto Calamelli and Leonardo Bettisi, known as 'Don Pino'. Both started from similar principles to those of the schools of Urbino and Casteldurante, but sought to revitalise traditional shapes by the introduction of new ideas of modelling and decoration. They took over the technique of producing white ware, which was to be the most influential in the next century. (According to the *Three Books on the Art of the Potter* by Piccolpaso, a writer from Casteldurante, this technique originated in Ferrara). Fine, white, cold enamels were used; they were left almost entirely undecorated except for scenes painted with only a few brush strokes in the *compendiario* technique. The result was reminiscent of the freshness and spontaneity of some ancient Roman wall paintings; and in particular grotesques, coats of arms and various floral motifs were handled very delicately. This was clearly a reaction to the imposing manner of the Urbino school, and indeed to all the earlier maiolica which had been entirely covered with *istoriate* scenes or intensely coloured decoration. It is possible that the creation of these white pieces was partly due to the renewed interest displayed in

22 Savona. Plate with figures of peasants, *c.* 1670.
Kunstgewerbemuseum, Hamburg.

23 Savona. Plate with border in relief. 17th century.
Museo del Castello Sforzesco, Milan.

22   Savona. Plate with figures of peasants, *c.* 1670. Kunstgewerbemuseum, Hamburg. Popular and genre subjects are very common on Savona pottery and are often derived from engravings of the 16th century. From Savona this fashion spread across Europe, especially influencing the French school of Nevers and the early ware of the Low Countries.

23   Savona. Plate with border in relief. 17th century. Museo del Castello Sforzesco, Milan. A typical example of a type of ware that was widespread in Liguria, thanks especially to the work of Guidobono. The shapes of the border are barely recognisable but their aim seems to be to imitate the rich embossed work of silverware.

24   Savona. Large plate with Susanna and the elders. 17th century. Museo Internazionale delle Ceramiche, Faenza. An interesting meeting-point with the art of Faenza, which towards the end of the 16th and throughout the 17th century had achieved in its 'white pieces' — wide modelled plates often decorated with bean motifs — a type of decorative maiolica which was highly effective. Even the style of painting, done with swift touches of the brush, is here derived from the *compendiario* style of Faenza.

25   Manardi workshop. Large plate with the meeting of Christopher Columbus and Queen Isabella. Museo del Castello Sforzesco, Milan. Comparison with the previous plate makes the derivation of certain pieces of Savonese pottery very clear. But in general the earliest pieces from the Veneto show a greater attention to detail and a more delicate, more varied range of colour. For many years the factory of the Manardi restricted itself to working infinite variations on this single theme.

24 Savona. Large plate with Susanna and the elders. 17th century. Museo Internazionale delle Ceramiche, Faenza.

25   Manardi workshop. Large plate with the meeting of
Christopher Columbus and Queen Isabella. Museo del
Castello Sforzesco, Milan.

Oriental porcelain at the time; but there can be little doubt that the main stimulus was provided by the Renaissance tradition itself. All the new development – the form of fluted dishes, the vases and bottles with slimmer lines and handles of only moderate projection, the preference for filigree and new shapes like obelisks, pyramids, lamps, busts and inkwells inspired by bronzes, and the impressionistic dappled technique of painting – were of the greatest importance in the future development of maiolica. The Ligurian school, for example, the most important in Italy for much of the 17th century, drew inspiration from this source, and many of the most successful decorative schools in Europe derived from Faenza's *compendiario* style.

The 17th century

The period of good Italian maiolica is generally believed to have ended at the turn of the 16th century. For some time during the early Baroque period, however, Italian workshops continued to produce good quality pieces which were often superior to the general European level. It was not until the full flowering of the French and Dutch workshops in the latter half of the 17th century that Italian ware became of secondary importance. The best examples of 17th century Italian maiolica represent logical developments from the ware of the schools of Faenza and Urbino. Even if most of them lack the distinction of earlier works, they are still comparable with works in other contemporary artistic forms.

Liguria and the Veneto were the most active Italian centres of the 17th century. Montelupo, which had inherited the traditions of Florence and Cafaggiolo, also produced some work of note; but its craftsmen relied heavily on standard stylistic ideas and an agreeable kind of pictorial decoration. The subjects were street characters, soldiers, duellists and galloping knights, and the prediliction of the craftsmen (or their customers) was for popular work that was both local and literary. A large part of this output has no more than amusement or curiosity value.

The influence of Urbino on the Ligurian school can be seen in many pieces. It can be seen in the great *Adoration* of 1576 (in the Chiesa della Concordia in Albisola), which was executed by one of the first workshops in Albisola, that of Agostino Salamone, in juxtaposed panels based on an Urbino design; the magnificent tiled floors and walls at Savona (they were once in the Porticato and the Palazzo dei Pavesi, but are now broken up); and the panels in S. Maria di Castello Genoa. This tendency had its source in Albisola, where the workshops of Salamone, Seirullo, Grosso and Siccardi were all busily employed in making the large range of pharmaceutical vases of Albenga, Savona and Genoa. These workshops exploited the complete repertory of Urbino and Faenza but adopted a linear, calligraphic style of decoration.

From its precise linear decoration the school of Savona soon evolved a new conception expressed in clear, continuous shapes. In this it was following the example of the white ware of Faenza and, even more, the fine contemporary Genoese silverware. The repetition of types for pharmaceutical use naturally continued; several complete sets are still in existence. The potters of Savona and Albisola are distinguished by the originality of their invention, their modelling, and their free style of painting, which gives the impression of a spontaneous creative urge. In this they were following the trend towards free, fantastic shapes characteristic of the Baroque. The white ware of Faenza was the point of departure, in particular the ware in which shapes and ornamentation were varied, as in the early 17th-century works of Stefano Accarisi and Francesco Vicchi. The early Savona potters executed wonderfully imaginative pieces, using brightly coloured paint, very often light-blue, and adopting a swift, sketchy style of painting. Admittedly the pieces sometimes appeared to have been

26 Angarano. Plate with ruins and a statue of Hercules.
17th century. Museo Internazionale delle Ceramiche, Faenza.

26 Angarano. Plate with ruins and a statue of Hercules. 17th century. Museo Internazionale delle Ceramiche, Faenza. Another typical example of Angarano ware, though utterly different from the preceding one. The early Romantic taste for ruins in a landscape is characteristic of much of the painting of the time: in the present case a comparison can be made with the work of the landscapist Marco Ricci.

27 Bernard Palissy. Oval dish with animals in high relief. Victoria and Albert Museum, London. This is one of a large group of similar pieces doubtfully attributed to Palissy. To the same potter are also attributed plates decorated in detailed, elegant relief with mythological and allegorical subjects related to the style of the school of Fontainebleau and at times inspired directly by the work of Benevenuto Cellini, who was then well known in France.

28 Nevers. Vase with mythological figures. 17th century. Victoria and Albert Museum, London. Still connected with the Savonese tradition as regards the style of figuration, this vase — which dates from the middle of the century — has a new elegance of shape that is certainly derived from Far Eastern pieces, which became known at Nevers at a remarkably early date.

29 Nevers. Flask. 17th century. Victoria and Albert Museum, London. In this piece too, made about the middle of the century, it is easy to see the mixture of elements from the Savonese tradition — evident in the swift sketching of the figures as well as the landscape — with others from the Middle East (particularly from Persia), such as the shape of the article itself and the costume of the figures shown on it.

27 Bernard Palissy. Oval dish with animals in high relief.
Victoria and Albert Museum, London.

28 Nevers. Vase with mythological figures. 17th century.
Victoria and Albert Museum, London.

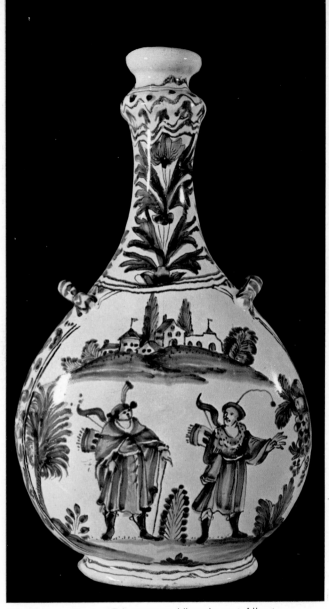

29 Nevers. Flask. 17th century. Victoria and Albert
Museum, London.

executed so quickly as to be almost careless. The Chiodo family worked in this style with greater finesse, and before long their French colleagues in Nevers and Moustiers had made detailed copies in their dishes with scenes based on the fashionable prints of Antonio Tempesta, Callot and Stefano della Bella. This 'sketchy' style was followed in France and Italy until the end of the century despite its mannered and artificial elegance.

The most prolific family in the second half of the century was that of Guidobono – Giovanni Antonio and his sons Nicola, Bartolomeo and Giovanni Bartolomeo (called 'the priest of Genoa'). Besides pharmaceutical equipment, their workshop produced large dishes painted in light-blue enamels. These may have been inspired by silver, but they, in effect constituted an original artistic form owing to the way in which relief work and painted ornamentation merge. The decoration sometimes consisted of light bean-motif patterns of the kind of filigree work typical of Faenza at the end of the 16th century, but sturdy volutes, painted shells in large medallions and cherubs were more often employed. The painting, in *compendiario* style was of sea-gods, nymphs, tritons and winged cherubs. The jugs, mugs and vases were decorated with the bean-motif in the manner of beaten metal, and were covered with festoons in relief.

The ware produced by the Guidobono workshop was decisive in the development of Ligurian maiolica. Its styles were copied by the Valente and by the workshops of Albisola, as can be seen from the works of the Corrado family, who gave a fresh Italianate stimulus to the school at Nevers, where they worked. Throughout the century Liguria maintained its reputation for strong, vigorous modelling, though it was eventually overwhelmed by the German and French taste in decoration. These sculpturesque products had an influence on another important Italian workshop, that of the Manardi brothers at Angarano near Bassano. At first this workshop, founded in 1669, imitated only Faenza white ware; but gradually it turned to Savona, using the exuberant ornamentation of Savona to decorate its own (infrequently produced) vases, and in particular the trellis-like borders in relief of its plates. The Manardi specialised in the production of a limited range of plates, which were renowned for the extreme delicacy of their pictorial decoration, though their form never varied. At the centre are landscapes, painted in extremely subtle colours, which are superb copies of the views of a contemporary from Bassano, Marco Ricci. They include ruins, romantic landscapes with shepherds, and deserted houses set in the middle of clumps of trees. This exuberant decoration often spreads to the edges of the plates. At times it can be seen in perfectly shaped oval tiles designed for wall hanging; maiolica tiles had a precedent in Delft, which had by now become the leading centre of European tin-glazed ware.

Any consideration of maiolica as a background for pictorial scenes would be incomplete without some mention of another Italian family – that of Carlo Antonio Grue, who worked in Castelli, a small town of the Abruzzi. Grue managed to create an entirely individual type which was to have great success in southern Italy and became very popular in Naples at the beginning of the 18th century. He covered his plates, jars and tiles with scenes taken from well-known paintings of the 16th and 17th centuries. These included Madonnas and other religious subjects by Federico Barocci and Ludovico Carracci, grotesques in the Flemish style, and landscapes of all kinds from marine landscapes to views of ruins midway in style between the Dutch 'Roman' artists and the Classical school. Grue's range was enormous, and was extended still further by his sons Francesco, Anastasio, Aurelio and Liberio, each of whom was a specialist in his own line. The last of the family, Saverio, was active to the end of the 18th century. The work of the Grue family always reached a high level, but the motifs they employed became standardised; the colour range hardly varied, the artists mainly relying on the same striking mixture of yellows and intense blues, and of deep orange and pastel green.

The 18th century

Although Italy was a cultural tributary of France during the 18th century, its traditional pottery centres maintained their output. The new European taste for the graceful and refined was catered for but not felt, and Rococo forms were accepted as unavoidable rather than from deep-rooted conviction.

At first sight it seems strange that Italian art was in the long run scarcely influenced by art from the Middle and Far East, though it had been in contact with this art far earlier than any other country. Venice, for instance, had helped to spread Oriental styles, and both France and Florence in the 15th and 16th centuries had employed a decorative style known as *alla porcellana*. Yet it was in other European countries that Oriental influence had brought about the profound changes which led to the phenomenon of chinoiserie. Perhaps the cause lay in the undisputed sway in Italy of the artistic theories of the Renaissance;

30 Nevers. Jug. 17th century. Victoria and Albert Museum, London.

30   Nevers. Jug. 17th century. Victoria and Albert Museum, London. Executed towards the end of the century. This jug is one of the earliest examples in which the motif of bunches of flowers appears on a blue ground. The motif itself — which is sometimes displayed on a yellow ground — became widely popular throughout France (at Rouen and Marseille in particular) in the following century.

31   Rouen. Plate, c. 1680. Musée des Arts Décoratifs, Paris. A fine example of Chinese taste harmoniously combined with the kind of rich, minute 'embroidery' decoration typical of this school. The colour is relatively sober, avoiding over-lively or brilliant effects; while the drawing evinces extreme refinement and subtlety of line.

32   Rouen. Plate with chinoiserie, c. 1680. Musée des Arts Décoratifs, Paris. Another fine example of decoration freely inspired by Oriental styles. The motifs of several different Chinese 'families' are here united, and the colour takes on a brilliance which is not generally found on the original Eastern items.

33   Rouen, about 1680. Water-jug. Musée des Arts Décoratifs, Paris. A typical helmet-shaped vase with decoration like embroidery. The sobriety of its relief and colour is far removed from the character of similar pieces of the Italian Renaissance, from which it derives. It polygonal shape and very precise decorative style are derived from the East.

31　Rouen. Plate. *c.*1680. Musée des Arts Décoratifs, Paris.

32 Rouen. Plate with chinoiserie, *c.*1680. Musée des Arts
Décoratifs, Paris.

33 Rouen, about 1680. Water-jug. Musée des Arts Décoratifs, Paris.

but more likely it was the greater refinement and elegance that European culture had acquired. Chinese porcelain and Japanese lacquer were exotic in European eyes, and furthermore their delicacy and their amusing subjects were bound to appeal to a cultivated aristocratic society. By contrast, Italy had experienced neither centralisation nor the preponderant influence of court life, and was therefore at a grave disadvantage compared with, say, France.

Despite their lack of original ideas and their dependence on imported designs, Italian maiolica centres continued to function with considerable success. At Lodi, the factory of the Coppellotti – founded by Antonio but at its best under his son Antonio Giovanni Maria – broke with tradition by introducing the whole range of French pottery into Italy. The styles of the late Baroque were abandoned in favour of simple, shapes enriched with sumptuous but refined decorative painting. The Rouen *en broderie* style, chinoiserie and grotesques *à la Bérain* were all copied with effect. The younger Coppellotti tended to overburden his works, covering them entirely with decoration, but he did create various motifs which gave him a distinctive style. Antonio Ferretti and Giacinto Rossetti followed a similar path. They enlarged their repertory with motifs that were more obviously Rococo, such as paintings of flowers in bunches or the only moderately effective *a fiamma* (flame motif). The Lodi factories were immediately successful. In 1721 Rossetti founded a prosperous business in Turin where the Rococo style was greatly developed together with earlier kinds of decoration. Two other Lodi potters, Antonio Casali and Filippo Antonio Callegari, were active in Pesaro for many years from 1763.

The far more original Milanese factories of Felice Clerici and Pasquale Rubati reached their peak slightly later. Clerici began about 1745 and first gained distinction for his many accurate copies of Japanese vases of the Imari-Arita period. He was also notable for a kind of earthenware decorated with azure edges and subjects derived from chinoiseries, pastoral Rococo and scenes of everyday life. His Chinese *magots* are different in spirit from similar European pieces since they contain an element of ironical Lombard humour. Rubati was also interested in Oriental forms, but he is particularly noted for his beautifully decorated services with roses in relief coloured in vivid reds, blues and greens.

At Nove in the Veneto, Giovan Battista and Pasquale Antonibon, and later (just after 1800) Giovan Maria Baccin followed the fashions of the Rococo. Following the trend set by Marseille and

Strasbourg, they concentrated on *'trompe l'oeil'* earthenware in the shape of fish or cabbages. At the end of the 18th century the Modenese Geminiano Cozzi, already famous for his porcelain, produced a range of maiolica ware in Venice which eclectically followed prevalent fashions, including Rococo, chinoiseries and French floral decoration.

Models from north of the Alps soon superseded local traditional work at Genoa, though a *compendiario* type of decoration remained characteristic of this school, derived from the Chiodo family, which reached heights of free energetic brilliance. Miniature landscape decoration (often confused with chinoiserie) became very popular, as did fountains and Rococo vases decorated with bunches of flowers. Giacomo Boselli, who had worked at Marseille, reproduced in eclectic styles all the models of the time from English earthenware to early Neo-Classical pieces. He was a versatile potter who displayed considerable sensitivity in choosing his decorative subjects, and he worked from the paintings of such leading Genoese artists of the period as Agostino Ratti and Gian Tommaso Torteroli.

The fashionable styles were also adopted at Faenza. About 1780 the painter Filippo Comerio designed emerald green chinoiserie silhouetted on a

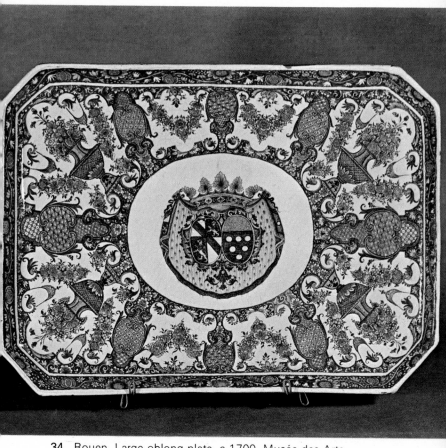

34 Rouen. Large oblong plate, *c.*1700. Musée des Arts
Décoratifs, Paris.

35 Rouen. Plate, *c.*1700. Musée des Arts Décoratifs, Paris.

36 Rouen. Plate, *c.* 1700. Victoria and Albert Museum,
London.

34   Rouen. Large oblong plate, *c*. 1700. Musée des Arts Décoratifs, Paris. Here is the festoon motif (*à lambrequins*) which was the favourite decorative device of the French factories, lasting right into the Neo-Classical era. It has been employed in this case to break up the painted area into small elements.

35   Rouen. Plate, *c*. 1700. Musée des Arts Décoratifs, Paris. The relief which is here given to the central area and the shape of the coat of arms supported by lions appear to be derived from a type of plate produced in Holland — particularly in the workshop of Pijnacker — and taken up again by the craftsmen who were working at Canton commissioned by the Dutch.

36   Rouen. Plate, *c*. 1700. Victoria and Albert Museum, London. This is an example of the 'radiant' (*rayonnant*) style of decoration. Notice how the design of the decorated part has been subjected to a rigid, almost geometrical structure, so as to make the whole appear kaleidoscopic.

37   Rouen. Jug. 18th century. Musée des Arts Décoratifs, Paris. In this little jug, whose style tends to the popular and which was made about halfway through the century, the naturalistic motif of flowers is stylised according to an Oriental pattern. The same type of decoration is found in the very same period in German factories, especially at Hanau and Nuremberg.

37 Rouen. Jug. 18th century. Musée des Arts Décoratifs, Paris.

white ground for a range of articles remarkably similar to Hannong products. (They too were fired in a 'muffle' kiln.) This was in the Ferniani factory, which also produced pots, decorated with bunches of flowers on a yellow ground, resembling the successful products of the Perrin factory at Marseille.

SPAIN

Throughout the 16th and for most of the 17th century Italian maiolica dominated European pottery, and the work of Italian artists spread to even the remotest parts from the beginning of the 16th century. Their impact did not always have a fundamental effect and their work remained isolated owing to failure to establish their method securely in local traditions. The real importance of Italian influence, certain and lasting though it was, takes on a new aspect when it is remembered that in the middle of the 17th century when the French and Dutch schools were beginning to produce their richest work, they had already turned to quite different ranges and established a very clear gap between the new designs and the old.

In Spain the tradition of Moorish tin-glazed ware

persisted for an extraordinarily long time. The name maiolica itself derived from the island of Majorca, which acted as a clearing house for this kind of work. Typical examples of Spanish work were the great blue-decorated basins with ivy leaves symmetrically arranged and finished with metallic-toned golden lustres. The secret of manufacturing these was long sought for in Italy, and they were still influential in Italy and the rest of Europe as late as the early 16th century. The use of tin-glazed earthenware tiles (*azulejos*) to decorate floors and walls, which was adopted in Spain in imitation of the fabulous shining Arab tiles, became familiar throughout Europe and gave rise to the fashion of completely covering walls or floors with them. The Italians adopted the practice chiefly for religious decoration, but in the Low Countries it was developed to a high degree. The centres of this art were originally Catalonia and Andalusia, later Valencia and Manises, and later still almost the whole Mediterranean coast of Spain. The tiles were decorated with polychrome enamels, and at first the *cuerda seca* technique was employed, i.e., with greasy lines outlining and separating areas of colour; later the *cuenca* technique was adopted, by which the pattern was impressed upon the tile, the ridges so formed keeping the colours apart.

According to Vasari, della Robbia sent work to Spain. Then, early in the 16th century, Francesco Niculoso Pisano brought to Seville a treatise on the new figurative style in Italy. He transcribed the small figured tiles of the Faenza tradition on a huge scale in several great sets of decorative tiles, of which notable examples are the panel of 1503 on the tomb of Inigo Lopez in the church of St Anna and that of 1504 on the altar screen of the Alcazar. Pisano's somewhat Flemish and hybrid style varies between a typically Hispano-Moresque way of covering the tiles and the Italian tendency to adapt this kind of decoration to an illusionistic spatial composition. Pisano's work in Seville is not really of great significance.

At the beginning of the 17th century there was a further echo of Italian art, this time in Castile. Here the work of Talavera, which has been described as Italo-Flemish, closely followed the motifs used at Savona, with its painting of stylised leaves and birds and its boldly painted landscapes with mythological scenes. The work of Talavera closely followed that of the rest of Europe until the emergence in 1726 of the factory of Alcora, whose ware was very much akin to that of Moustiers (largely because of the presence of French artists). Elsewhere in Spain geometrical motifs of Arab origin continued to be used throughout the 17th century by a number of not very distinguished workshops.

THE LOW COUNTRIES

Throughout the 16th century craftsmen in the Low Countries were strongly influenced by Italian tin-enamelled wares. Before 1600 the earthenware of Antwerp was inspired by Venetian models, stimulated perhaps by the style of paving in the Abbey of Herckenrode (now in the Musée d'Art et d'Histoire in Brussels). This was created by Pier Francesco da Venezia in 1532, and consisted of square tiles painted with animals, busts and palm leaves in the Faenza style. Other motifs in the Italian styles, such as grotesques, were learned from prints. Early in the 16th century an artist from Casteldurante, Guido Savini (or Andriesz) settled in Antwerp. He was the head of a large family of potters who worked in several places in Holland and also in England.

In Holland, Italian influence at first merged with the Moresque tradition and Eastern elements; but the Delft workshops soon left these styles behind, achieving an accomplished and noble style of their own which was based on wonderfully refined and

38 Moustiers. Plate with hunting scene. 17th century.
Musée des Arts Décoratifs, Paris.

38 Moustiers. Plate with hunting scene. 17th century. Musée des Arts Décoratifs, Paris. A typical end-of-the-century example of a hunting plate inspired by Antonio Tempesta's prints. Often the same scenes are reproduced on more than one article, as is the case here: some years ago there was a tray in the Arnavon Collection in Paris with exactly the same scene.

39 Moustiers. Tray. 18th century. Musée des Arts Décoratifs, Paris. Executed in the early years of the century. The tray is decorated in the style known as *à la Bérain*, in which the pattern of the decoration is subjected to a principle of strict symmetry. Despite the fact that Bérain was not a potter, he owes a good deal of his fame to pottery, which spread his discoveries all over Europe.

40 Moustiers. Upper part of a fountain. 18th century. Musée des Arts Décoratifs, Paris. This piece dates from the mid-century and is decorated with *lambrequins*, as is the lower part (not shown here), which consists of a large basin. The festoon motif had its greatest success in porcelain, on which it was repeated without variation for several decades.

39 Moustiers. Tray. 18th century. Musée des Arts
Décoratifs, Paris.

40 Moustiers. Upper part of a fountain. 18th century.
Musée des Arts Décoratifs, Paris.

precise painting rather than inventiveness. One of the basic designs of this Delft 'blue' school, so called because it is painted entirely in shades of monochrome blue, is a plate of simple shape with a white or figured edge and a large surface area for painting. Another basic design was a simple, smooth rectangular tile painted all over. Both plates and tiles were products of good schools whose outstanding artists were Frederick von Frijtom and Abraham de Cooge.

Although this 'Delft' ware drew upon the Italian *istoriate* style and the monochrome colouring of Chinese porcelain, the result was a style of great originality. The painted scenes, which included mythology, landscapes, Old Testament scenes, hunts, beasts, battles, figures and portraits, were executed with the delicate skill of the miniaturist. Dutch art, which had found new values in the intimate poetry of everyday life depicted in dignified and sober colours, was one of the main sources of inspiration.

From the beginning of the 17th century, Chinese porcelain was widely imitated in Holland. This continued throughout the 18th century despite the fact that from about 1710 comparable work was being done elsewhere in Europe on porcelain itself, the manufacturing secrets of which had at last been discovered by Böttger at Meissen. In Italy, Oriental porcelain had occasionally been copied as early as the 16th century, but during the 17th century the Dutch East India Company (founded in 1602) brought in large quantities which stimulated the demand for Chinese and Japanese plates and vessels. All over Europe, but above all in Holland, potters attempted to compete in this market, which of course led to a great extension of the range of delftware, the craftsmen reproducing all the colours and styles of the original Chinese and Japanese plates and vases. These ranged from large vases of polygonal section to round ones on a high base; from monochrome decoration with stylised flowers to polychrome and gold genre subjects; and from green decoration with 'reserves' – white oval spaces in which flowers and leaves were usually painted – to exotic birds. Oriental silks had begun to appear in Europe, but since their subtle, indefinite patterns made stylistic discrimination difficult, potters moved haphazardly from the Ming dynasty of China to the Imari ware of Japan and the decorative style of Indian materials. And at the same time they invented shapes which were freely inspired by the East so that by about 1660 the close imitation of Oriental ware began to evolve into a new style and generate a new taste – for chinoiserie as opposed to Chinese art.

The art of the Far East inspired many artists around the turn of the 17th century, among them Albrecht de Keise, Gerit Pieteresz Kam, Adrianus Kocks, Samuel and Lambertus van Eenhoorn, Rochus Hoppesteyn (with whom the painter Gijshreckt Verhaast worked) and Louvys Fitoorsz. They were all specialists in copying the many styles of Oriental porcelain including Arita ware in polychrome and gold, known as delft dorée, and a form of green and yellow decoration on a black ground which was a speciality of Pieter Poulisse and Adriaen Pijnacker.

During the 18th century delftware was surpassed and overwhelmed by the porcelain of Meissen and Sèvres. Attempts to compete by imitating them merely led to sterility. Much the same process was taking place in almost all other European countries; the foundation of the Meissen porcelain works in fact dealt a heavy blow to tin-glazed ware, whose creators from then on had to struggle to survive at all. Delft, Haarlem and Amsterdam produced an enormous quantity of articles, ranging from traditional pieces to statuettes, *magots* (statuettes of Chinese divinities in meditative poses), animals from the East and all kinds of French decoration. The memorable pieces of the period are those by Gerrit Brouwer decorated with *trompe l'oeil* playing cards.

41   Marseille. Plate with Perseus and Andromeda (detail), *c.*1690. Musée des Arts Décoratifs, Paris.

41   Marseille. Plate with Perseus and Andromeda (detail), *c.* 1690. Musée des Arts Décoratifs, Paris. The plate is a product of the oldest factory in Marseille, that of St Jean du Désert. It still shows the influence of the Italian *istoriate* style, although the regular division of the border painted with landscapes is new.

42   Marseille. Plate and Jug. 18th century. Musée National de Céramique, Sèvres. In the 18th century the workshops of Marseille produced many examples of Rococo shapes decorated with highly imaginative but light and charming patterns. These pieces demonstrate the level of perfection reached in the pottery both technically and aesthetically.

43   Marseille. Tray in the style of Tempesta. 18th century. Musée National de Céramique, Sèvres. An octagonal tray with a symbolic pastoral scene depicted with precision of detail. This is a typical product of the factory of St Jean du Désert.

44   Strasbourg. Earthenware bowl in the shape of a cabbage. 18th century. Musée des Arts Décoratifs, Paris. A typical example of the illusionistic style very common not only in Strasbourg but in Marseille and Italy as well. Besides cabbages, fish shapes were frequently made, and there were even 'duck' and 'boar's head' bowls.

42   Marseille. Plate and Jug. 18th century. Musée National
de Céramique, Sèvres.

43 Marseille. Tray in the style of Tempesta. 18th century.
Musée National de Céramique, Sèvres.

44 Strasbourg. Earthenware bowl in the shape of a
cabbage. 18th century. Musée des Arts Décoratifs, Paris.

The practice of covering walls with tiles had passed from Spain to Holland before the latter had thrown off Hapsburg rule. Tiles were widely used not only to decorate walls but also floors, chimneys and the façades of houses. In Holland the Italian decorative motifs of the 16th century gave way in the 17th to freer forms decorated in polychrome or turquoise monochrome boldly applied on a white ground. Traditional subjects were used, though the execution was generally bolder and more free. The style was mainly created at Rotterdam and Amsterdam, becoming distributed throughout Europe.

During the first half of the 18th century the Dutch tile was in wide use in palaces and castles from Hampton Court to Versailles, from Bavaria to Denmark. As a result, workshops producing similar ware arose in Poland, South Germany, Switzerland, Austria and Italy. This production was especially favoured in the 19th century, when there was a fashion for enormous tiled chimneys.

FRANCE

The contribution of the Italian masters to the flowering of the French School was even more important.

During the reign of Philip I a member of the della Robbia family, Girolamo di Andrea, restored one of the great royal houses on the Ile de France, the Château de Madrid, which is unfortunately no longer in existence. Artists from Forli, Cafaggiolo and Florence worked in Lyons, Amboise and Brittany at the turn of the 15th century; and in the second half of the 16th century the links became even stronger when artists from Pesaro, Faenza and Genoa crossed the Alps. Some of them enjoyed the patronage of Henry III, who created centres for the production of faïence in Paris, Nevers and Brizambourg in 1580. Orders for Faenza ware were frequent, and Cardinal de Touruon of Lyons interested himself in the work of Urbino mainly through Piccolpasso's treatise on the subject. It was in France that Renaissance maiolica was most appreciated, just as it was France that welcomed Italian artists like Cellini, Rosso and Primaticcio.

The first independent French productions, in about 1550–70, were those of Bernard Palissy and St Porchaire of the lower Loire. Palissy decorated the Tuileries grotto for Catherine de Medicis. Although the work is lost, a few extant fragments make it possible to attribute a large series of plates decorated in high relief and polychrome to Palissy. The decoration is after the manner of della Robbia, in which knots of serpents, lizards, toads and fish are depicted with a slightly repellent, almost surrealistic effect. They are close to the cruel, sophisticated death scenes of Antoine Caron, exemplifying an approach to reality typical of Mannerism.

The rare pieces of St Porchaire are more conventional by comparison. The style of Urbino is given a new edge by a kind of symmetrical, precise decoration which seems to foreshadow the almost geometrical ormentation of Rouen. The contemporary ware of Lyons, on which was used white clay covered only by transparent paint, displays somewhat similar characteristics.

Nevers did not free itself quickly from the Italian influence, which was particularly powerful there because some members of the Corrado family of Albisola settled there soon after the arrival of Luigi Gonzaga, who was Duke of Nevers from 1566. In sculptures which were clearly della Robbian and in showpieces which followed Urbino and Liguria, the Renaissance mood remained until the middle of the 17th century. After this there was a gradual return to more slender pieces with delicate decoration in a manner similar to that which prevailed in Holland. In fact Nevers' reversion to a more refined style of vase possibly derives from the Dutch imitation of

45 Holland. Plate. 17th century. Victoria and Albert
Museum, London.

Eastern work and the monochrome blue decoration of Delft. Nevers vases, attributed to the factory of Pierre Custode, had small round bodies and high swelling necks which showed the influence of the Persian shapes which had become known in Venice. Persian art was enjoying a great vogue at this time, and through it the appreciation of Islamic forms was enhanced.

Nevers also produced ware in the 'Franco-Nivernais' style, craftsmen ransacking the whole range of contemporary painting and engraving for the decoration of plates much as the schools of Delft and Liguria did at about the same time. The Franco-Nivernais school produced a variety of much larger articles inspired by China or Japan.

It must again be stressed that products of this sort were more than good imitations of Oriental porcelain. In Holland and France only faithful copies of Chinese and Japanese originals were made at first, but with the development of a taste for chinoiserie the original was transformed into an autonomous form with its own particular aesthetic. It was not a slavish imitation like the later copying of European porcelain, but the expression of a clearly defined taste.

This was particularly true at Nevers, which did not have the competitive character displayed, for

46 Delft. Imitation Chinese vases, *c.*1700. Musée National de Céramique, Sèvres.

45 Holland. Plate. 17th century. Victoria and Albert Museum, London. An example of the earliest Dutch ware, which faithfully imitates Italian models. The shape of this plate is a clear reminder of the fluted plates of Faenza, and the decoration seems to be descended from that type called *alla porcellana* because of its affinity with Oriental models.

46 Delft. Imitation Chinese vases, *c*. 1700. Musée National de Céramique, Sèvres. The shapes of these pieces are directly inspired by those of Chinese ware. All three — which were originally destined to decorate a chimney-piece — show complete freedom in the figured area with motifs of naturalistic flowers.

47 Delft. Plate with the Return of the Prodigal Son. 18th century. Musée National de Céramique, Sèvres. It was common practice at Delft to paint Biblical scenes on ware for domestic use. The uniform blue is typical of the school, which manages to overcome the absence of colour by a truly exceptional pictorial virtuosity.

47 Delft. Plate with the Return of the Prodigal Son. 18th century. Musée National de Céramique, Sèvres.

example, by Delft in relation to the porcelain imported by the Dutch East India Company. In Nevers ware at the end of the 17th century a point can be discerned at which the Oriental archetypes are transmuted into models of the French Baroque. This was a manifestation of the supreme sense of proportion and order which characterises Classicism north of the Alps. The pictorial decoration of the pieces, rendered with thread-like fineness, is arranged with extreme care. Ornamental and figured bands alternate and are in turn divided into regular geometrical elements. Floral decoration with areas on which landscapes and genre scenes are painted becomes increasingly abstract and falls into an almost preordained pattern. Nevers ware is a forerunner of products of the later and more famous French factories at Rouen, Moustiers, Marseille and Strasbourg.

The faïence produced at Rouen is even more directly related to French culture. Just as early in the 16th century Italian maiolica had been inspired by motifs which were more in vogue as wall decorations, so French faïence found a source of inspiration in contemporary articles which reflected the culture of the court at Versailles. Ornament like embroidery, which was produced at Rouen and elsewhere, is reminiscent of wrought iron, gold- and silver-work, even of contemporary landscape design. It is the evident result of an inclination towards symmetry characteristic of French Classicism.

Although Rouen made an Italianate start (for the shop of Poterat long followed the Faenza *compendiario* style), the factories of Pierre Heugue, Guillibaud, Bertin, Levasseur, Paul Caussy, Pinon de Breards, Etienne Bouttin and Pierre Chapelle made great use of the traditional Chinese 'families' copied in Holland. They adapted them to their own ends, interposing figurations within simply modelled shapes and with a logically and rationally designed decorative pattern. In a more original vein there were superb decorative motifs in rays (*style rayonnant*) and festoons (*lambrequins*) which developed the manner of Nevers even further while ridding it of all excess in colour and pattern. The rare and distinctive rather than grave shapes are Renaissance work purged of every superfluity. The colour, generally of delicate shades, seems to articulate the shape rather than emphasise the decoration, which is in turn rich without being obtrusive. The Rouen style requires that every element shall balance every other element.

Craftsmen at Rouen did not in fact renounce richness in their decorative motifs, which spread over each piece like some delicate embroidery (whence the name of the style, *en broderie*). Although some of the common decorative types of the Italian Renaissance, such as the familiar *a quartieri* design, were precursors of this style, a comparison will show the originality of the Rouen ware. Whereas the Italian craftsman imitates painting by attempting to reproduce reality, the later artist is primarily concerned with line, creating a network of tracery that becomes an abstract entity.

The new world of French potters neatly avoided any culture. It is clear how Chinese art was easily able to hold its own and find its place in the current fashion by virtue of its imaginative invention, however abstract, and above all by its measured and controlled expression.

The new Rouen style of 1690–1756 created many shapes, though these were products of a series ·of variations upon given themes rather than completely new types. The usual shapes of bottles, water-jugs like upturned helmets, cache-pots, plates and immense monumental vases, were repeated with variants that made each piece unique. At the same time the use of certain decorative motifs – grilles, volutes, festoons, wreaths, palm-leaves and grotesques – did not lead to the establishment of 'families' since they were constantly permutated.

The Rouen style found favour elsewhere, exercising a profound influence upon Moustiers, Marseille and Strasbourg, although they all followed very different paths. By breaking with tradition the ornamentation employed at Rouen created the meticulous, sober taste which lasted until the advent of Neo-Classicism soon after the middle of the 18th century. Evidence of this influence is the popularity throughout the Neo-Classical period of the festoon, which first appeared on Rouen vases, and the use of light ornament raised in relief on a white ground, which also originated at Rouen.

At Moustiers the great exponents of 17th-century faïence were in the workshops of the Clérrisy (where painters like de Viry worked), who were later to start a pottery in Marseille. Early Moustiers ware follows the *istoriate* style, drawing inspiration from the whole range of subjects then fashionable, but especially hunting scenes, which they treated largely in the late Mannerist style. This was probably because of the availability of hunting prints, particularly those of Antonio Tempesta. As the century advanced, the finer Rouen style made its impact and aroused a desire for calligraphic decoration. The shapes of the pieces became simpler and the decorators abandoned *chiaroscuro* in favour of the Rouen *en broderie*.

48 Frankfurt. Jug, *c*.1700. Kunstgewerbemuseum, Vienna.

49 Holitsch. Mars, *c.* 1750. Kunstgewerbemuseum, Vienna.

48 Frankfurt. Jug, *c.* 1700. Kunstgewerbemuseum, Vienna. An example of popular pottery, especially in the simplicity of its shape. The decoration, with a landscape in vaguely Chinese style, derives from Dutch delft. Most German faïence of this period consists of jugs (*kanne*) and cylindrical mugs (*krug*).

49 Holitsch. Mars, *c.* 1750. Kunstgewerbemuseum, Vienna. Hungarian ware does not reveal much originality. In this case the maker is clearly inspired by the porcelain figurines so common all over Europe at the time — the most famous being those of Kändler at Meissen, not to mention those executed at Frankenthal, Chelsea, etc.

50 Westerwoldt. Amphora with decoration in relief. 17th century. Victoria and Albert Museum, London. A typical piece of German art. This amphora is called a *ring-krug*, and is descended from a 16th-century group (*Töpferfamilie knütgen*). The most original German pottery is of precisely this kind; a group of amphoras and mugs with decoration in high relief but entirely without pictorial decoration.

51 Ludwigsburg. Triangular plate. 18th century. Musée National de Céramique, Sèvres. In Ludwigsburg, as elsewhere in Europe, the same factories produced porcelain and pottery, and generally employed the same shapes as well as the same decorative styles. On this fine example of faïence the light decoration in garlands is the same as that used in Ludwigsburg upon porcelain.

50 Westerwoldt. Amphora with decoration in relief. 17th
century. Victoria and Albert Museum, London.

51 Ludwigsburg. Triangular plate. 18th century. Musée
National de Céramique, Sèvres.

The particular style chosen by Moustiers within the general trend was decoration *à la Bérain*, which became widely popular and was imitated everywhere. Jean Bérain was a well-known painter who continually devised new decorative motifs which were adopted by everybody from potters and tapestry weavers to painters (particularly those concerned with interior decoration, since his ideas stemmed from ancient murals). His purpose was to purify the Italian grotesque of every too-allusive or too-realistic element. His grotesques, while making use of the full repertory of sphinxes, fauns and imaginary animals found in the Raphaelite grotesque, reduced the decorative element to an interlacing of fine lines executed in rigidly symmetrical patterns; this often framed mythological scenes. The ornamentation now included some of the elements typical of the Rococo. Plates in this style reveal the fine taste of Rouen with their rhythmical, restrained tracery and Oriental-influenced abstract designs. Later, from about 1738, Joseph Olerys, also of Moustiers, produced pieces full of the most varied contemporary influences: the motifs range from chinoiserie to decoration with garlands in the style of Rouen, from genre subjects based on Callot prints to variants on flat trophies in Rococo style.

Throughout the 18th century pottery was enriched

by potters' efforts to keep up with the expansion of the porcelain industry. This induced most factories to adopt the technique of firing in a 'muffle' kiln at a low temperature, which permitted greater control of the gradation of colour in relief and the use of more delicate shades. Clérissy's early (pre-1680) Marseille workshop at St Jean du Désert was closely connected with the early Moustiers and Nevers products and produced *istoriate* plates still in the style of Tempesta and chinoiserie in the Rouen manner. Low-temperature firing was also used at Marseille, at the factories of Perrin, Robert and Bonnefoy, which concentrated on plates, vases and other articles decorated with elegant animated, Arcadian scenes. After following the Rouen style from 1720–50 the Hannong factory at Strasbourg perfected a new technique involving a double firing system which enabled it to produce an unrivalled wealth of decorative motifs. Gilding began to be used for decoration at Strasbourg in 1744. From Strasbourg a naturalistic style of painting with various kinds of multi-coloured European flowers – originally practiced as Meissen – spread and became widely imitated. Both Marseille and Strasbourg were famous for tureens in the form of huge animals, fishes and cabbages or other vegetables.

Among the most famous of the other factories in

France were Niderviller, remembered for its Lemire statuettes and *trompe l'oeil* decoration imitating grained wood and cards, and Sinceny, Sceaux and Lille. These factories have several aspects in common. The range of products during the 18th century was vast. It included new products such as *tulipières* and candlesticks, wig boxes and pans of every shape, *magots*, *potpourris*, coffee-pots, scent-burners, knife-handles, fountains, sacred and profane statues, stoups and crucifixes. The aid of faïence and porcelain, as of all art, was being increasingly sought to assist in the beautifying of houses and transforming the appearance of functional articles. The range of figurative decoration was similarly extended, since each new kind of piece was immediately reproduced or imitated by other factories. The decorative types of the Middle and Far East and every hybrid form between them and contemporary art was to be found. There were naturalistic and *trompe l'oeil* motifs, Rouen arabesques and festoons, Moustiers grotesques and Italian historical and landscape scenes.

This diffusion of motifs was encouraged by the many handbooks of prints which, together with engravings, spread them to the remotest parts of Europe. Such volumes had first begun to circulate in the 16th century, and in the next two centuries they

52 Marieberg. Tureen. 18th century. Musée National de Céramique, Sèvres.

53 Germany. Perfume burner. 1765. Kunstgewerbemuseum,
Vienna.

52   Marieberg. Tureen. 18th century. Musée National de Céramique, Sèvres. A piece similar to the preceding one. In Marieberg, the greatest Swedish pottery in the 18th century, pottery and porcelain were produced together in the same styles, chiefly inspired by those of the French schools. The factory itself was founded and for a long time directed with the collaboration of famous French craftsmen like Pierre Berthevin.

53   Germany. Perfume burner. 1765. Kunstgewerbemuseum, Vienna. Produced in Franconia. This perfume burner displays the elegant Rococo elements which characterised French porcelain in its play upon volutes and cartouches.

54   Germany. Stove. 1773. Kunstgewerbemuseum, Vienna. The fashion for large porcelain stoves was Dutch in origin but in the 16th and 17th centuries spread all over northern Europe, including northern Italy. This stove was painted by Abraham Leihamer, an artist who specialised in painting flowers and landscapes on faïence. He was active in north Germany at Kiel, Eckenforde and Stockelsdorf.

55   Grue family. Plate with rustic allegory. Museo di S. Martino, Naples. Although executed by one of his sons, probably Francesco Saverio, this plate is a typical example of the work of Antionio Grue, the Abruzzese artist who worked for a long time in Naples. The subjects painted by Antonio were always set in extensive landscapes of an Arcadian pastel green. Even the edges always repeat the same designs.

54   Germany. Stove. 1773. Kunstgewerbemuseum, Vienna.

55 Grue family. Plate with rustic allegory. Museo di S. Martino, Naples.

achieved remarkable popularity and importance. Cotelle's *Nouveau Livre de Chenest* (1700), Bérain's *Ornamenti* (1709) and Messionier's Oeuvres (1709) were notable examples. Motifs intended for soft fabrics and silverware were immediately copied in the other arts. The eclecticism of 18th-century taste played a part in this distribution of patterns, but the basic reason was the industrial organisation of the French factories, of which there were hundreds by the middle of the 18th century: competition prevented a factory from limiting its range to a few typical shapes. As a result, new decorative ideas appearing on glass or silverware were transcribed with amazing rapidity.

The one thing which conditioned the majority of pieces being produced was European porcelain. If, as has been suggested, every historical period has an art that perfectly expresses its character, there is little doubt that porcelain embodies the 18th century. Drawing rooms were entirely furnished with it from pier glasses to candlesticks and bric-à-brac because it was at once precious and aristocratic., Porcelain was an indispensable element in the wealthy household in a way that faïence had never been, despite the admiration of the Renaissance nobility.

This was an evil omen for an art which had for decades run the risk of declining in attempting to provide substitutes for other materials. Exhibition ware rivalled the gold- and silverware from which it had drawn inspiration, plates and panels followed the example of painting, and floors, walls and chimney pieces were decorated with earthenware tiles. To all this could be added new types derived from porcelain shapes, trinkets, tobacco boxes, cutlery handles, mirror frames, lamps and circular statuary with allegorical and mythological themes and portraits.

Halfway through the century faïence began to participate in the Rococo – the typical porcelain style, although it originally stemmed from painting and sculpture. Tureen shapes became undulating, cartouches and volutes were rife, pastoral and chivalrous themes became commonplace. The change was noticeable in Rouen, Moustiers, Marseille and Strasbourg, as in the rest of Europe. In order to perfect the imitation of porcelain, craftsmen everywhere resorted to low-temperature firing and many, like Hannong, began gilding their works.

The struggle could not be maintained for very long. The Free Trade treaty of 1786 and the consequent invasion of English earthenware quickly ended the splendid flowering of French faïence, and a period of decline began.

ENGLAND AND GERMANY

The history of tin-glazed ware in England is somewhat barren. 15th-century English ware consisted mainly of simple, uniformly painted mugs which were only occasionally decorated with geometrical lines in an elementary manner. Such objects never amounted to much more than purely utilitarian ware for the lower classes. The Cistercian style, even simpler in shape, is of no greater interest. Some Continental influence was inevitably felt. The floor of Vyne Castle (1520), for example, appears to have been the work of Guido di Savino of Casteldurante, who was then active in Antwerp; and certainly artists from Antwerp are known to have been in London and Norwich by about 1750. The most productive English centre was Lambeth, but no works are known which display any signs of maturity, let alone quality.

England was one of the countries in which the craze for chinoiserie was strongest, and the influence of Chinese art is found in English pottery even earlier than in Holland. Ware produced under the influence of Dutch and Chinese art began to appear in England about 1750. Production was centred on Lambeth and Bristol, but still lacked variety and refinement. Styles which had long been abandoned elsewhere, such as the

56 Felice Clerici. Plate with lovers. Museo del Castello
Sforzesco, Milan.

57 Pasquale Rubati. Plate with relief decoration of roses.
Museo del Castello Sforzesco, Milan.

56   Felice Clerici. Plate with lovers. Museo del Castello Sforzesco Milan. The creations of Clerici always vacillate, as in this example, between a lively observation of reality and an Arcadian, Rococo feeling for the pastoral. It was no accident that the characters of the Commedia dell'Arte were among his favourite subjects: they were themselves figures halfway between reality and fable.

57   Pasquale Rubati. Plate with relief decoration of roses. Museo del Castello Sforzesco, Milan. These services ornamented in high relief in brilliant but controlled polychrome colours were the speciality of Pasquale Rubati. Both Clerici and Rubati practised in Milan an eclectic art inspired by all the styles then in vogue – only to arrive at a style of their own which is unlike any other in Europe.

58   Antonio Ferretti. Plaque. Museo Civico, Lodi. The work of Ferretti, like that of all the masters of Lodi, was somewhat eclectic. Here he is following the style with sprays of flowers that originated in Strasbourg but soon appeared on pottery and porcelain all over Europe. The sensitive handling of the paint is very striking and the piece has an undeniable freshness.

59   Savona. Vase. End of the 18th century. Palazzo Rosso, Genoa. At the end of the 18th century, Savona renounced their ancient tradition and turned to the imitation of northern European models. The only sign of the place of origin of this vase is the vitality of the free technique employed for the decoration. This in turn has its origins in the painting of the Chiodo family.

58 Antonio Ferretti. Plaque. Museo Civico, Lodi.

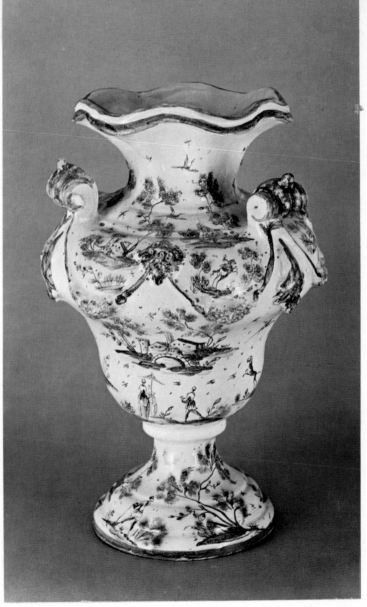

59 Savona. Vase. End of the 18th century. Palazzo Rosso, Genoa.

Italian *istoriate* style, still continued to be employed.

English pottery and porcelain reached its highest level late in the 18th century. The greatest originality was displayed not in tin-glazed ware but in slipware. The same forms were retained unaltered for nearly two centuries. This ware is admittedly a by-way in the history of ceramics, but its peasant connections were important in enabling many Medieval images to survive. Slipware is decorated with strips of white clay in relief or covered with slip (a clay mixture), through which a design is 'scratched' (*sgraffitto*). Human figures, dates and names are often to be found on such ware as well as allusions to proverbs and allegories. Most of the pieces were made to celebrate marriages, births, etc. One complete set found in London dates from the mid 17th century, but the most remarkable collection comes from North Staffordshire. Thomas Wedgwood was working there at this time, and there are many signed works of about the 1670s by Thomas Toft and members of the Simpson family.

Tin-glazed ware was quite widely produced in Germany. In the 18th century, Germany of course made her greatest contribution to ceramics, for it was the Meissen factory that produced the first pieces of European porcelain. The earliest faïence from Hamburg, Frankfurt and Potsdam was in the Dutch style in both its Eastern shapes and the decoration with religious subjects on a monochrome surface. This type of ware was produced until late in the 18th century. Occasionally some originality was shown – in Nuremberg, for instance, with its taste for thick, superabundant, though at times not very elegant decoration.

Open imitation gradually ceased during the 18th century, though Meissen porcelain remained closely linked to the decorative French style through its adoption of low-temperature firing. The styles included the Rouen type with garlands; chinoiserie and flower painting from Niderviller and Rococo. Meissen porcelain was also made at Nuremberg by J. Schäfer and W. Rössler, and at Bayreuth by A. F. von Löwenfinck. The biggest factories at Durlach, Künesberg, Höchst and Ludwigsburg (the last two of which were renowned for their porcelain), also remained faithful to the French and Dutch styles which entirely dominated the central and northern European markets. These styles were also imitated at Holitsch in Hungary, where two Frenchmen, Charles François Leduc and Nicolas Germain, worked, at Copenhagen, at Rörstrand and Marieberg in Sweden, and at Herrebøe in Norway.

60 Staffordshire. Plate with the figure of a siren. Second
half of the 17th century. Victoria and Albert Museum,
London.

61 Staffordshire. Plate with King William. 18th century.
Victoria and Albert Museum, London.

60   Staffordshire. Plate with the figure of a siren. Second half of the 17th century. Victoria and Albert Museum, London. Slip-ware was executed by applying thin strips of soft clay upon a base of different colour. This plate shows all the ingenuity of popular imagination. The name at the bottom, 'Thomas Toft', probably refers to the maker, otherwise unknown; another Toft (John) executed pottery of the same kind about a century later.

61   Staffordshire. Plate with King William. 18th century. Victoria and Albert Museum, London. Closely related to the previous example in technique and style. This kind of slipware has similarities with other forms of popular art in Germany, Austria and Bohemia. The name at the bottom, 'Ralph Simpson', is that of the maker.

62   Liverpool. Plate, c. 1750. Victoria and Albert Museum, London. This is executed in a fresh decorative vein, but is still influenced by the exotic Dutch models of some decades earlier.

62 Liverpool. Plate *c.*1750. Victoria and Albert Museum, London.

MODERN TIMES

Tin-glazed ware continued to be produced in the 19th century, but we are still too close to the period to evaluate its products with any assurance. Brosio comments, 'Perhaps the eclecticism of these years contributed to this – years which drew inspiration successively from the Classical world, the 17th- and 18th-century Baroque and the Romanesque and Gothic styles as well as from the Byzantine and the Egyptian.' The 19th century is in fact so eclectic as to lack a definite style, unless this romantic evocation of the past itself constitutes a definite style. The main difficulty of assessing 19th-century ware lies in the fact that it is not sufficiently differentiated from contemporary porcelain to constitute independent stylistic groups. Factories continued to use similar decorative motifs on both pottery and porcelain, though the pottery was intended for the general public (who were relatively undemanding) while porcelain was intended for aristocratic drawing-rooms. Since decoration could now be reproduced mechanically, the value of the single piece was lost. And of course, mass-production makes evaluation even more difficult.

In the 20th century pottery has undergone a

development comparable in certain respects with that of the Renaissance. Now, as then, a new kind of pottery is being produced in which concern for function has given way to a desire to make ceramics that are independent works of art. Contemporary painters and sculptors explore the vast range of opportunities afforded by this art; they have become fascinated by its almost infinite range of lustres, the brilliance of oxide colours and enamels, and perhaps most of all by the opportunity pottery offers of combining pictorial and sculptural aims. The current renewal of the art of pottery surely indicates a return to a sensitive art form which is deeply bound to a half primitive, half civilised form of expression. The combination of painting and sculpture in the early years of Western art suggests that an intellectual desire to separate the two is only dormant. Very few contemporary artists have not at some time or other applied their gifts to pottery; which is hardly surprising when one considers that it has entered the curricula of art schools and that many of the original pottery centres, for instance Faenza, Caltagirone and Naples, have been turned into public institutions.

The revival has been gradual. In Paris in 1907, for example, the potter André Metthey was encouraging some of the great artists of the day – Matisse, Rouault,

63   Romania. Plate. 18th century. Muzeul Satului, Bucharest.

64 Nuremberg. Jug. 1826. Musée National de Céramique,
Sèvres.

65 Herrenbøe. Tureen. 1834. Musée National de Céramique,
Sèvres.

63   Rumania. Plate. 18th century. Muzeul Satului, Bucharest. An example of popular craftsmanship. The common types in Rumania are often related to English slipware; but it is easy to see that the range of decorative motifs, consisting as it does of a few geometrical patterns and an element of stylised floral decoration is completely untouched by outside influences. This plate comes from a village in north-eastern Transylvania.

64   Nuremberg. Jug. 1826. Musée National de Céramique, Sèvres. German pottery always maintained a level of moderate quality, and repeated in the 19th century the fashions of the previous century. The shape of this jug and its type of decoration derive from Dutch art.

65   Herrenbøe. Tureen. 1834. Musée National de Céramique, Sèvres. The shape and decoration of this tureen are pure Rococo, and copy French models. The pottery of this Norwegian centre was characterised by an exaggerated taste for Rococo shapes, a taste which lasted — as in all the smaller centres in Europe — into the 19th century.

66   Bordeaux. Teapot. 1830. Musée des Arts Décoratifs, Paris. A fine example of pottery influenced by Neo-Classical porcelain. Its shape is extraordinarily close to that of Sèvres porcelain, which was still the dominant ware in Europe at this time.

66 Bordeaux. Teapot. 1830. Musée des Arts Décoratifs,
Paris.

Derain, Vlaminck – to paint his products; but the collaboration was short-lived. Later, Dufy, Miró and Braque painted many pieces by the Spanish potter Loren Artigas.

The revival has been more vigorous in Italy – and perhaps not by chance, since painters have had the opportunity to learn their trade in some of the original centres of maiolica; Arturo Martini in Treviso, for example, and Agenore Fabbri and Tullio d'Albisola in Albisola. In Italy ceramics are connected with a movement of liberation in the arts. The techniques of pottery have served many as an exercise in immediate expression and in swift flights of imagination in which colour plays a considerable part. Few contemporary Italian painters and sculptors have not handled clay at least once since 1945: Sassu, Manzù, Migneco, Scanavino, Garelli, Capogrossi, Cascella, Perilli and Leoncillo.

In England there is a distinguished school of studio-potters (Bernard Leach, Michael Cardew); in France two famous artists, Léger and Picasso, have made pottery. Picasso, like Martini and Fontana, was attracted by the existence of a local popular tradition, and he was particularly enthusiastic about it at Vallauris after 1946. Although it was only an episode in Picasso's artistic life (in any case a series of episodes),

67 Edouard Avisseau. Jug. Musée des Arts Décoratifs,
Paris.

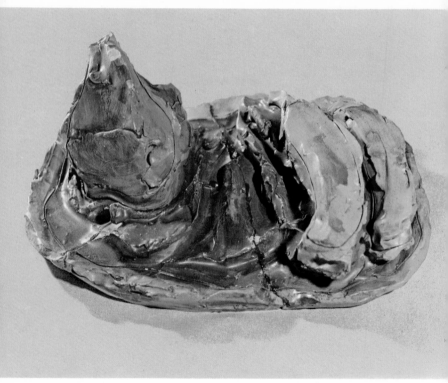

68 Lucio Fontana. Bananas and figs. Museo Internazionale delle Ceramiche, Faenza.

69 Marc Chagall. Plate with Abraham and the three angels.
Museo Nazionale delle Ceramiche, Faenza.

67 Edouard Avisseau. Jug. Musée des Arts Décoratifs, Paris. Many pieces from the last century reveal a rather eclectic taste. Here, for example, the vaguely Rococo shape is combined with emphatically naturalistic details such as the spray of leaves which covers the body of the vase. Avisseau worked at Tours in the second half of the century.

68 Lucio Fontana. Bananas and figs. Museo Internazionale delle Ceramiche, Faenza. In this piece, which is one of his earliest, Fontana exhibits a rich, opulent sense of form which he was to abandon in time. The pliancy of the clay and the ample opportunities for lively and brilliant colouring enable the sculptor to convey the fragrant sense of ripe, almost disintegrating fruit.

69 Marc Chagall. Plate with Abraham and the three angels. Museo Nazionale delle Ceramiche, Faenza. Here is another case of a famous artist of our time turning his hand to pottery; and certainly the slight indeterminacy and seemingly fortuitous shape and colours which only the baking clay can give, offer new opportunities to the dreamy and rarefied art of Chagall.

70 Picasso. Plate with a dove. Museo Internazionale delle Ceramiche, Faenza. The dove is one of Picasso's favourite themes; this piece was executed not long after 1950, so it may be considered one of his earliest pieces of pottery.

70 Picasso. Plate with a dove. Museo Internazionale delle
Ceramiche, Faenza.

he was probably drawn to pottery because it gave him the chance to effect some of his beloved metamorphoses – turning jugs and mugs into human and animal figures – as well as offering the possibility of executing colourful scenes. In his anthropomorphic vases Picasso has gone right back to the very origins of ceramic art and mastered it completely.

It would be useless to search 20th-century maiolica for the characteristic techniques that were handed down from Islamic times for its types and purpose are not what they were. This century has broken free from the need for an applied art which is not mass produced and which conceives the original article, of whatever type, without regard to its functions. It is characteristic of the time that each form is rediscovered when a new piece is made in it and there is not a traditional technique which has not been upset by the demands of every artist. It is impossible to categorise such works of art as Picasso's Capra or the painting of Gentilini. The latest pottery developments show, on the whole, a free choice exercised with discernment.

It is clear that in the 20th century potters have not wanted to perpetuate the style of their predecessors; the art has been revived on different lines by the need for a new kind of expression. The artists of this century have no point of contact with the potters of former times, who were intent on following traditional patterns and meeting the demands of their clients; and indeed few of them can be considered purely as potters. However, thanks to this development, pottery has started a new and different artistic cycle.

LIST OF ILLUSTRATIONS page

64 Nuremberg. Jug. 1826. Musée National de **140**
Céramique, Sèvres.

65 Herrenbøe. Tureen. 1834. Musée National de **141**
Céramique, Sèvres.

66 Bordeaux. Teapot. 1830. Musée des Arts Décoratifs, **143**
Paris.

67 Edouard Avisseau. Jug. Musée des Arts Décoratifs, **145**
Paris.

68 Lucio Fontana. Bananas and figs. Museo Inter- **146**
nazionale delle Ceramiche, Faenza.

69 Marc Chagall. Plate with Abraham and the three **147**
angels. Museo Nazionale delle Ceramiche, Faenza.

70 Picasso. Plate with a dove. Museo Internazionale **149**
delle Ceramiche, Faenza.